Platform Engineering
Essentials

Building Internal
Developer Platforms
for High Productivity

Taylor Royce

DEDICATION

To all the creative thinkers and unrelenting troubleshooters who work to advance technology. We are all inspired by your enthusiasm for developing practical and efficient solutions. This book is dedicated to people who think that internal developer platforms have the ability to revolutionize our working methods and that teamwork is powerful. I hope it will help you on your platform engineering journey and give you the tools you need to create a future with high productivity and smooth integration.

CONTENTS

ACKNOWLEDGMENTS

To everyone who helped create *Platform Engineering Essentials: Building Internal Developer Platforms for High Productivity,* I would like to extend my sincere gratitude.

I want to start by expressing my gratitude to my family and friends for their constant encouragement and support along this journey. Your confidence in me has consistently inspired me.

My knowledge of platform engineering has been substantially enhanced by the knowledge and experience of my mentors and coworkers, for which I am incredibly thankful. Your openness to sharing your expertise and experiences has influenced the book's content and motivated me to investigate novel concepts.

A particular thank you to the reviewers and early readers who offered priceless input. Your insights made the manuscript better and guaranteed that the ideas were applicable to today's technological environment.

Additionally, I want to thank all of the research papers, journals, and websites that have influenced my work. Innovation and knowledge in platform engineering are still fueled by the contributions of industry thought leaders.

Lastly, I want to thank my readers. This book exists because of your quest for knowledge and your drive to increase organizational productivity. As you traverse the always changing landscape of platform engineering, I hope the insights found inside these pages prove beneficial and transformative.

CHAPTER 1

AN OVERVIEW OF PLATFORM ENGINEERING

Platform engineering, which offers a unified approach to infrastructure, automation, and development processes, is quickly becoming a crucial component of contemporary software development. The definition, development, and fundamental ideas of platform engineering will all be covered in this chapter. Organizations may improve efficiency, scalability, and developer satisfaction by better aligning development and operational goals through a knowledge of the importance and structure of platform engineering.

1.1 Platform Engineering Definition

The creation, upkeep, and optimization of the "platform," or infrastructure layer, that facilitates software development are the core goals of platform engineering. It entails creating a collection of environments, frameworks, and tools that enable development teams to produce code reliably, securely, and swiftly.

The goal of platform engineering is to streamline and standardize processes, lower complexity, and give teams self-service access to key resources and procedures.

The following are the major responsibilities of this engineering domain:
1. Infrastructure provisioning and management.
2. Automating pipelines for deployment.
3. Enforcing compliance and security.
4. Tracking dependability and performance.

The main purpose of platform engineering teams is to support developers by offering them a unified, intuitive platform that abstracts away infrastructure complexity so they can concentrate on code and feature delivery.

Function and Significance in Contemporary Development Settings

Platform engineering has surfaced as a way to simplify

development pipelines as software development grows more complex due to diverse tech stacks, cloud resources, and security requirements. Important advantages include:

Increased Developer Productivity: Developers may now develop more effectively since they are not burdened by complicated configurations and dependencies.

Consistency Across Environments: Platform engineers lower the risk of deployment problems by establishing a standardized platform that guarantees consistent configurations across development, testing, and production environments.

Platform engineering facilitates scalability by creating standardized procedures that are simple to duplicate across teams and projects, creating a development environment that is both scalable and agile.

1.2 The Transition from Platform Engineering to DevOps

The transition from DevOps to platform engineering demonstrates a change in emphasis from teamwork to the development of standardized, developer-friendly environments. Development and operations are combined in DevOps, which developed techniques to produce dependable software, shorten development cycles, and enhance deployment frequency. But as the use of DevOps increased, new problems surfaced, and platform engineering developed as a logical solution.

Historical Background

In order to close the gap between development and operations, DevOps was founded in the early 2000s. It promoted automation, CI/CD pipelines, and infrastructure as code (IaC).

Although DevOps was successful in breaking down silos, teams still had to deal with bottlenecks relating to complicated settings and dependency management, which reduced productivity.

How DevOps Principles Are Extended by Platform Engineering

Standardization and Consistency: Platform engineering is concerned with offering a standardized platform that unifies tooling, processes, and configurations between teams.

Platform engineering places a strong emphasis on self-service platforms, which let developers access resources and services on their own, whereas DevOps promotes automation.

Developer-Centric Design: Platform engineering is developed with developers in mind, producing user-friendly platforms that abstract difficult operational chores, in contrast to DevOps, which focuses on integrating development and operations.

1.3 Platform Engineering Fundamentals

Platform engineering's fundamental tenets developer autonomy, consistent settings, and a focus on standardization are what make it so effective. Every concept helps create a collaborative development atmosphere and a more efficient development process.

Self-Service

Offering self-service features to developers is one of the fundamental principles of platform engineering. Platform engineering makes it possible for developers to access resources like databases, infrastructure, and CI/CD tools without requiring help from operations teams by creating automated workflows and intuitive user interfaces. **Important elements consist of:**

Ease of Access: There is little difficulty for developers to access and configure resources.

Platform engineering uses automation to produce scalable, repeatable solutions that developers can use whenever they need them.

Decreased Dependency: Self-service makes developers less dependent on operations teams, which speeds up deployment and eliminates bottlenecks.

The process of standardization

In order to guarantee consistent development environments and lessen the possibility of differences between development, testing, and production, standardization is essential. Platform engineering encourages predictability and dependability by implementing standardized procedures and instruments. Among the elements of standardization are:

Establishing the same set of tools and procedures that all teams utilize, such as logging, monitoring, and CI/CD pipelines, is known as "unified tooling."

Standardizing configurations across environments to prevent problems with environment-specific faults is known as "configuration management."

Decreased Complexity: Platform engineering reduces the learning curve for novice developers and increases the predictability of the development process by ensuring standardization.

Centric Design for Developers

With the developer experience in mind, platform engineering produces platforms that are easy to use, intuitive, and optimized for workflows. Platform engineering facilitates more effective development and problem-solving by putting developer needs first. **Important characteristics include:**

User-Friendly Interfaces: Dashboards and developer portals that facilitate resource management, deployment, and viewing.

Extensive Documentation: Comprehensive instructions, templates, and examples that facilitate developers' rapid onboarding and troubleshooting.

Feedback Loops: Platform engineers collaborate closely with developers to integrate feedback, ensuring that the platform is continuously improved to satisfy changing requirements.

The advantages of core principles

Platform engineering offers a solid basis for quicker development, scalability, and security by following these guidelines. These guidelines encourage creativity while striking a balance with the requirement for operational effectiveness:

Accelerated Development Cycles: Developers may concentrate on delivering features as self-service tools and standardized environments cut down on wait times.

It is simpler to implement security standards and keep an eye on compliance across environments when procedures are standardized. This leads to improved security and compliance.

Improved Developer Satisfaction: Engineers have a better experience when a developer-centric strategy that emphasizes self-service, consistency, and ease of use is implemented.

Platform engineering, which provides an organized method that incorporates DevOps best practices while resolving its drawbacks, is quickly becoming essential for contemporary software development teams. Organizations may recognize how platform engineering is a potent enabler for effective, scalable, and developer-friendly software development environments by defining its tenets and comprehending its development.

CHAPTER 2

THE FUNCTION OF INTERNAL DEVELOPER PLATFORMS (IDPs)

The requirement for specialized infrastructure to support development workflows grows as businesses get bigger and more sophisticated. This need is met by Internal Developer Platforms (IDPs), which offer a unified, controlled environment that simplifies resource access, speeds up development, and lessens conflict between teams. This chapter examines the foundations of IDPs, how they affect developer productivity, and the key elements that make them successful.

2.1 What is a Platform for Internal Development?

By offering a centralized, self-service environment where developers can access resources, deploy code, and maintain applications with little operational overhead, an internal developer platform (IDP) is intended to expedite the development process. By serving as a liaison between development teams and the underlying infrastructure, IDPs free up engineers to concentrate on building and deploying code rather than handling intricate infrastructure needs or configuration management.

Definition and Essential Elements

Typically, an IDP consists of a few essential elements that combine to provide a complete and approachable solution:

1. In order to enable developers to provision resources as needed without depending on operations of DevOps teams, IDPs provide them with self-service access to resources like databases, compute power, and storage.

2. **Unified Interface:** IDPs offer a single, standardized interface that enables developers to carry out operations like deployment, scaling, and monitoring from a single location. This interface is frequently provided by a web portal or command-line interface (CLI).

3. **Automated Workflows:** Code is efficiently moved through the development, testing, and production

phases thanks to built-in automation features like continuous integration and continuous deployment (CI/CD) pipelines.

4. The ability of IDPs to abstract infrastructure difficulties frees developers from worrying about the underlying hardware, network, and other infrastructure specifics, enabling them to work with a higher-level representation of resources.

5. **Observability and Monitoring:** An IDPs real-time monitoring, logging, and alerting features provide developers with insight into the health and performance of their applications, enabling proactive problem solving.

2.2 IDPs' Advantages for Developer Efficiency

IDPs are effective instruments for increasing developer productivity, enabling teams to produce features more quickly and with fewer mistakes. IDPs simplify workflows and remove bottlenecks that frequently impede development by standardizing procedures and facilitating simple access to necessary resources.

Main Advantages

1. **Time Savings:** IDPs enable developers to operate without the assistance of operations teams, cutting down on waiting times for permissions or resources. Developers can deploy code, run up environments, and access required tools whenever they need them thanks to self-service capabilities.

2. **Decreased Errors:** Automated procedures in an IDP, like standardized configurations and pre-configured CI/CD pipelines, reduce the possibility of human error. IDPs lessen the possibility of deployment mistakes and environment mismatches by enforcing consistency and best practices.

3. **Streamlined Processes:** IDPs create a clear path from development to production by streamlining and consolidating workflows, removing unnecessary steps. The developers can concentrate on high-value jobs like coding and testing because of this simplified method, which lessens their cognitive load.

IDPs Enhance the Developer Experience

IDPs offer user-friendly interfaces and efficient workflows that improve the entire experience, all while keeping developer comfort in mind. The following are important elements that enhance the development experience:

1. **Consistent Development Environments:** IDPs guarantee consistent development, testing, and production environments by standardizing configurations, which cuts down on debugging time and guarantees dependable performance across environments.

2. IDPs facilitate improved communication between development, operations, and quality assurance teams by providing centralized access to tools, logs, and metrics. This facilitates issue resolution and simpler handoffs.

3. IDPs offer a flexible platform that can adjust to shifting resource requirements as teams and applications grow, making it simpler to handle expanding user bases and sophisticated applications without requiring significant redesigns.

2.3 Foundations of Successful IDPs

IDPs need to have a number of fundamental components that facilitate durability, scalability, and seamless integration in order to fulfill their promise. Organizations may design strong IDPs that facilitate development at scale and give engineering teams a seamless experience by integrating these basic components.

The fundamental components of IDPs

One essential element of successful IDPs is automation, which makes it possible for code to move seamlessly from development to production. In an IDP, automation consists of:

1. CI/CD Pipelines: Code integration, testing, and deployment are streamlined by pre-configured pipelines, which minimize manual involvement and guarantee regular release cycles.

- **Infrastructure as Code (IaC):** IDPs simplify the process of provisioning, updating, and replicating environments in a consistent and automated manner by specifying infrastructure configurations as code.

- **Automated Rollbacks and Recovery:** Automation makes it possible to roll back changes instantly in the event of an error, minimizing and promptly resolving any production interruptions.

2. Observability

For teams to maintain performance and dependability, observability is crucial for tracking and comprehending application behavior in real-time. Important observability characteristics of IDPs consist of:

- **Logging and Monitoring:** Developers can keep an eye on the health of their applications, diagnose problems, and improve performance with the help of comprehensive logs and performance data.
- **Alerting and Notifications:** IDPs with integrated alerting features let teams know about possible problems so they can react and mitigate them quickly.
- **End-to-End Tracing:** Distributed tracing helps developers identify bottlenecks and improve application performance by giving them insight into the full lifecycle of requests.

3. Scalability: Scalability is necessary to adjust to growing user demands, workloads, and organizational expansion. Dynamically scaling resources without interfering with processes or necessitating a great deal of manual configuration is a feature of effective IDPs:

- Applications can scale up during periods of high demand and down during periods of low demand thanks to IDPs' ability to allocate and deallocate resources as needed.

- IDPs should allow both horizontal and vertical scalability in order to meet the needs of various applications. Horizontal scaling involves adding new instances, while vertical scaling involves increasing resource capacity.

- **Multi-Environment Support:** Teams may create and test features in isolated environments with IDPs that support several environments (such as staging and production), which makes deployment and scaling easier.

4. Compliance and Security

In order to keep data and apps safe from risks, security is crucial in any IDP. Standards for security and compliance are enforced throughout the development pipeline by efficient IDPs:

- Only authorized users are granted access to particular resources and actions within the IDP thanks to role-based access control (RBAC) and identity management.

- **Policy Enforcement:** To guarantee adherence to organizational and industry standards, IDPs enforce regulations on deployments, configurations, and data processing.

- **Auditing and Reporting:** IDPs with auditing skills offer thorough documentation of operations, assisting firms in maintaining regulatory compliance and spotting possible security threats.

Lastly, an efficient IDP places a high priority on a developer-centric strategy, ensuring that the platform is user-friendly, accessible, and built to promote productivity:

- IDPs should provide user-friendly interfaces, such as dashboards or portals, that make it easier for developers to access, deploy, and monitor resources.

- **Detailed Documentation:** Developers can maximize the platform's functionality with the help of thorough, well-structured documentation and guidelines, which lowers the need for assistance.

- IDPs are regularly improved to meet the changing needs of developers and remain in line with their processes by integrating user feedback.

By combining tools, automating processes, and offering developers a smooth environment, internal developer platforms are essential to contemporary software development. Organizations may use these platforms to boost development, increase productivity, and improve the developer experience by knowing the advantages, features, and components of an effective IDP.

CHAPTER 3

THE FUNDAMENTAL ELEMENTS OF PLATFORM ENGINEERING ARE COVERED

Designing, constructing, and maintaining an ecosystem that optimizes software development and operational procedures is the core goal of platform engineering. Platform engineering depends on a number of essential elements that streamline, automate, and enhance infrastructure management and software delivery in order to satisfy the demanding requirements of contemporary development environments. In order to improve productivity, lower errors, and facilitate effective scaling, this chapter explores the essential elements of platform engineering, such as Infrastructure as Code (IaC), CI/CD pipelines, monitoring, and observability.

3.1 Code for Infrastructure (IaC)

A fundamental idea in platform engineering, Infrastructure

as Code (IaC) allows teams to define, deploy, and manage infrastructure using code, simplifying and standardizing infrastructure installations. IaC speeds up the provisioning process, decreases human error, and increases consistency by enabling infrastructure to be provisioned and maintained as software. By giving developers and operational teams a common language, it also improves cooperation and version control.

Streamlining and Standardizing Configurations for Infrastructure

IaC defines infrastructure declaratively or imperatively using code. Engineers can declare the desired state of infrastructure (such as a virtual machine with a specific configuration) using declarative IaC tools like Terraform or Kubernetes YAML files, and the tool will handle getting the infrastructure to that state. Imperative IaC solutions, like Ansible, give teams greater precise control over infrastructure management by offering detailed instructions for configuring resources. IaC provides a number of important advantages:

- **Consistency Across Environments:** IaC minimizes

differences that may cause deployment problems by guaranteeing that infrastructure configurations stay the same across development, staging, and production environments.

- **Automated Provisioning and Scaling:** Teams can use IaC to automate resource creation and scaling as required. This feature is especially helpful in dynamic settings where demand-driven resource adjustments are necessary.

- **Version Control:** Teams may monitor changes, restore earlier configurations, and work together on infrastructure enhancements by storing infrastructure code in version control systems (like Git). This method produces a trustworthy change history that facilitates compliance and debugging.

- The ability to reuse IaC templates or modules across projects allows for speedier deployments and guarantees that best practices are performed consistently across several teams or applications. This is known as **Reusability and Modularity.**

The Best IaC Practices in Platform Engineering

Platform developers follow best practices that guarantee

dependability, scalability, and maintainability in order to maximize IaC:

- To ensure predictable results, make sure IaC scripts are idempotent, which means they can be executed again without introducing unexpected changes.
- **Modularization:** To make complex infrastructure easier to manage and to make IaC code more readable, divide it into reusable modules.
- **Continuous Testing:** Make sure infrastructure code functions as intended by implementing automated tests for IaC scripts to find configuration problems prior to deployment.

3.2 Pipelines for CI/CD

Platform engineering relies on pipelines for Continuous Integration (CI) and Continuous Deployment/Delivery (CD), which enable quicker and more dependable software releases. By automating the processes of integrating code changes, testing, and software deployment, CI/CD pipelines drastically lower the possibility of human error and manual intervention. Development teams may release code more frequently and with greater confidence thanks to CI/CD, which increases their agility.

Improving Delivery and Continuous Integration for Quicker Releases

Multiple steps make up CI/CD pipelines, and each one has distinct tasks meant to validate and implement code changes:

- Code updates are regularly incorporated into a common repository during the Continuous Integration (CI) stage. Every integration starts automated testing, which makes it possible to find errors and compatibility problems early. This procedure enhances code quality by enabling developers to quickly find and fix problems.

- **Continuous Deployment (CD):** Tested code modifications are automatically rolled out to a production environment during the CD stage. Teams can produce features more quickly thanks to this procedure, which reduces manual intervention. Organizations occasionally choose for Continuous Delivery, in which code is ready for deployment automatically but needs human approval before being made public.

Important Elements of a CI/CD Pipeline

Several steps in a well-designed CI/CD pipeline guarantee code quality, security, and performance:

- **Automated Testing:** Before code changes are deployed, automated tests, such as unit, integration, and performance tests, confirm that they adhere to quality requirements.
- **Build and Package:** To guarantee consistency across environments, code is compiled, built, and packed, frequently into containers.
- **Code Analysis and Security Scanning:** Static code analysis and security scans assist in locating coding flaws or vulnerabilities that may affect security or stability.
- For version control and tracking purposes, built artifacts, such Docker images or binaries, are kept in a repository.
- **Deployment to Multiple Environments:** Teams can verify performance in a test environment prior to

going live by deploying code to both staging and production environments.

The Best Practices for CI/CD in Platform Engineering

Platform engineers adopt these recommended practices to optimize the effectiveness and dependability of CI/CD pipelines:

- **Parallel Testing:** To expedite feedback loops and validate code modifications, run tests in parallel.
- To enable teams to version and reuse pipeline configurations across projects, define CI/CD pipelines as code using tools such as Jenkins, GitLab CI, or GitHub Actions.
- **Rolling and Canary Deployments:** Teams can distribute updates to a portion of users prior to a full release by using sophisticated deployment techniques like rolling and canary deployments, which decrease risk and downtime during upgrades.

3.3 Observability and Monitoring

Because they offer real-time insights into the functioning

of applications and infrastructure, monitoring and observability are essential elements of platform engineering. While observability offers a deeper understanding of complex systems through the collection, analysis, and visualization of data from multiple sources, effective monitoring enables teams to detect and address problems proactively. Platform engineers can ensure high availability, maximize performance, and react swiftly to problems when monitoring and observability are combined.

Facilitating Instantaneous Understanding for Quick Troubleshooting

Observability and monitoring provide multiple levels of insight into the health of networks, infrastructure, and applications:

- **Monitoring:** This entails keeping tabs on parameters such as error rates, request delay, memory utilization, and CPU usage. By configuring alerts according to thresholds, teams may react quickly to urgent problems.
- **Logging:** Logs enable comprehensive

documentation of transactions, failures, and events, providing important information for troubleshooting and comprehending system behavior. Logs are very helpful for tracking down incidents and determining their underlying causes.

- Distributed tracing, which helps teams find bottlenecks and improve service-to-service interactions, follows a request's path via various services in a microservices architecture.

- Response times, throughput, and system load are just a few examples of the quantitative information that metrics offer on system performance. Teams may see patterns, identify irregularities, and maximize resource utilization by combining and displaying metrics.

Putting Observability and Monitoring into Practice Effectively

Platform engineers concentrate on crucial tactics that improve system visibility and responsiveness in order to develop a strong monitoring and observability framework:

The use of centralized platforms, such Prometheus,

Grafana, or ELK Stack (Elasticsearch, Logstash, Kibana), can ease analysis and troubleshooting by guaranteeing that all metrics, logs, and traces are available in one place.

Faster incident response is made possible by configuring alerts according to performance thresholds or certain fault patterns. By integrating alerts with incident management software such as PagerDuty or OpsGenie, teams may effectively coordinate and address problems.

In order to match observability efforts with business objectives and user expectations, it is necessary to define Service-Level Objectives (SLOs) and Service-Level Indicators (SLIs) in order to set and monitor performance requirements, such as uptime and latency.

Optimal Methods for Observability and Monitoring in Platform Engineering

Platform engineers adhere to best practices for thorough monitoring and observability in order to optimize insights and facilitate efficient troubleshooting:

- Utilize instrumentation to ensure thorough coverage

by equipping infrastructure and applications with monitoring tools and libraries to record pertinent metrics and traces.

- **Create Useful Alerts:** that prevent alert fatigue, set up notifications that only sound when something actionable happens. Prioritize notifications based on severity levels to guarantee that urgent problems are addressed right away.

- **Continually Evaluate and Improve:** Review and update dashboards, thresholds, and monitoring metrics often to account for system modifications and changing business requirements.

Platform engineering makes it easier and more efficient for teams to manage complex systems by combining Infrastructure as Code, CI/CD pipelines, monitoring, and observability. These essential elements enable businesses to retain high-caliber software, increase development speed, and promptly adjust to shifting needs. They serve as the foundation for a robust, scalable, and developer-friendly platform that gives engineering teams the confidence to innovate and produce value.

CHAPTER 4

DELIVERY OF APPLICATIONS AND PLATFORM ENGINEERING

Platform engineering is essential to improving application delivery because it bridges the gap between operations and development to improve automation, streamline processes, and guarantee dependable, high-quality software. Organizations may improve the developer experience, decrease bottlenecks, and expedite the development lifecycle by coordinating platform engineering techniques with application delivery objectives. With an emphasis on workflow optimization, automation, and quality assurance, this chapter examines the essential elements of platform engineering in application delivery.

4.1 Simplifying the Process of Development

Making the development process simpler and faster is one of platform engineering's main objectives. The infrastructure, tools, and resources required to create and launch applications with little reliance on operations personnel are made available to developers in a self-service environment through Internal Developer Platforms (IDPs). IDPs provide a consistent interface for development tasks and standardize and consolidate resources, which lowers the friction frequently involved with setup and configuration.

How to Use IDPs to Speed Up Application Delivery

Platform engineers concentrate on a few crucial phases in the development process to expedite the delivery of applications:

Building a Unified Interface: An IDP allows developers to access all of their tools, environments, and resources from a single interface. Time spent hopping between many tools and platforms is decreased by this concentration.

Automating Setup and Configuration: IDPs automate routine operations related to setup and configuration, including resource provisioning, dependency management, and environment creation. Engineers can concentrate more on coding and less on setup by eliminating manual tasks.

Empowering Developers with Self-Service Options: Without assistance from the operations staff, an efficient IDP enables developers to carry out tasks like provisioning environments, executing tests, or deploying to staging. This self-service feature speeds up the development process and lessens dependency bottlenecks.

Standardizing Development Practices: Platform engineering contributes to uniformity in the development, testing, and deployment of applications by establishing standard configurations and best practices inside the IDP. Collaboration between teams is made easier and errors are decreased by this uniformity.

Encouraging Quick Feedback Loops: Real-time feedback tools like automated testing and alerting are part of an effective IDP because they let developers to spot and fix problems early in the development cycle. Higher-quality code and quicker development cycles are two benefits of rapid feedback loops.

Streamlined development workflows provide several advantages.

Workflows that are more efficient increase output, decrease context switching, and facilitate quicker, more frequent releases. Other advantages consist of:

1. Shorter time to market for updates or new features
2. Reduced problems related to environment and configuration
3. Improved cooperation between the operations and development teams; uniformity across environments and projects, which facilitates troubleshooting and lowers mistakes

4.2 Automation's Impact on Delivery Efficiency

The key to increasing delivery efficiency is automation. Platform engineering reduces manual involvement and enables teams to deliver features quickly and reliably by using automation to handle repetitive, time-consuming processes inside the application delivery pipeline. Testing, deployment, and feedback loops are just a few of the phases where automation is used to assist make sure apps fulfill quality and performance requirements prior to going into production.

Automating Feedback Loops, Deployment, and Testing

In platform engineering, automation typically encompasses three main areas:

Automated Testing: Before code changes move forward in the pipeline, automated tests, including unit, integration, and end-to-end tests, make sure they meet functional and performance requirements. Teams can identify problems early and lower the chance of bugs making it to production by automating testing. The CI/CD pipeline's continuous testing instantly validates the quality of the code.

Automated Deployment: This technique uses tools and scripts to transfer code changes from development to production with the least amount of human involvement possible. Deployment processes like environment configuration, resource scaling, and container deployment are made easier by tools like Jenkins, GitHub Actions, and Kubernetes. Platform engineering lowers deployment risk and time by automating these processes.

Automated Feedback Loops: These systems give programmers instant access to information on the stability and performance of their code. Dashboards, alarms, and monitoring tools that indicate faults, performance metrics, and other data from deployed applications are examples of these loops. Quick feedback ensures a more streamlined and dependable release cycle by assisting teams in recognizing and resolving problems as soon as they appear.

The benefits of automating the delivery of applications

Several significant advantages result from automating the application distribution process:

1. **Increased Speed and Reliability:** Delivery cycles are accelerated and human mistake is less likely when automated procedures run reliably.
2. **Resource Efficiency:** Teams may concentrate on higher-value activities like innovation and troubleshooting rather than manual deployment or testing by automating repetitive operations.

3. **Improved Consistency:** Automation makes sure that every pipeline stage adheres to the same procedures, increasing dependability and lowering errors.

4. **Enhanced Scalability:** Teams can manage more deployments thanks to automation, which facilitates scaling as projects get more complicated.

4.3 Using Platform Engineering to Ensure Quality

Maintaining the quality of apps is just as crucial as speed and efficiency. In order to guarantee that applications function as intended in production settings, platform engineering incorporates techniques that maintain code integrity and dependability. Engineering teams may identify and fix problems early by concentrating on platform quality management, which results in a more reliable and stable application delivery process.

Preserving Reliability and Code Integrity

Platform engineering offers procedures, guidelines, and tools to support dependable apps and high-caliber code.

Important procedures consist of:

The implementation of code reviews and automated tools, like static code analyzers, guarantees that code eliminates security risks, complies with coding standards, and follows best practices. This phase fosters teamwork in addition to maintaining code quality.

Static and Dynamic Testing: While dynamic tests verify code behavior while it is running, static analysis tools examine code for possible problems without actually running it. These techniques aid in ensuring that apps are secure and functional when paired with security testing.

Platform engineering places a strong emphasis on maintaining consistency throughout the development, staging, and production environments. By guaranteeing that code operates consistently across environments, this parity lowers the possibility of "it works on my machine" problems and minimizes production problems and deployment surprises.

Service-Level Agreements (SLAs) and Error Budgets:

SLAs establish performance standards, whereas error budgets enable teams to strike a compromise between dependability and innovation. Teams can maintain a healthy balance between development pace and quality by giving stability enhancements precedence over new features if error budgets above a predetermined threshold.

Methods to Preserve Platform Engineering Quality

Platform engineers frequently use these tactics to maintain quality:

1. **Shift-Left Testing**: Platform engineering helps teams find and fix problems early by relocating testing earlier in the development process, which lowers the amount of bugs that reach production.

2. **Canary and Blue-Green Deployments:** These deployment techniques reduce the risk of new releases by distributing updates to a subset of users ahead of a full release or by implementing changes gradually.

3. **Comprehensive Monitoring and Observability**: Platform engineering teams may identify and address problems promptly by continually

monitoring applications in production, guaranteeing that they satisfy performance and availability requirements.

4. **Creating Cycles of Continuous Improvement:** Platform engineering fosters a culture of continuous improvement, where teams examine and streamline procedures on a regular basis to resolve inefficiencies and technological debt.

By optimizing processes, utilizing automation, and upholding strict quality standards, platform engineering provides a strong foundation for enhancing application delivery. Platform engineering accomplishes these goals by lowering development pipeline friction, providing developers with effective tools, and guaranteeing that applications fulfill reliability and performance requirements. Platform engineers help companies create software more quickly, reliably, and with higher quality by concentrating on these fundamental ideas, which eventually makes the development environment more agile and competitive.

CHAPTER 5

ENHANCING THE SELF-SERVICE PLATFORM EXPERIENCE FOR DEVELOPERS

Self-service platform adoption is revolutionizing the developer experience by facilitating quicker, more independent workflows. Without depending heavily on the operations of DevOps teams, self-service platforms give developers immediate access to the infrastructure, tools, and resources they need to create, test, and launch apps. By eliminating bottlenecks and increasing productivity, this autonomy frees developers to concentrate on innovation rather than administrative challenges. This chapter examines how to reconcile developer freedom with organizational control, how to build self-service platforms that improve the developer experience, and how lowering reliance on operations benefits the entire development lifecycle.

5.1 Developing Developer Self-Service Choices

The purpose of self-service platforms is to provide developers with greater command over their work environment. Self-service platforms let developers carry out necessary tasks—like allocating resources, setting up environments, installing apps, and controlling access—on their own by offering a simple, user-friendly interface. Self-service alternatives decrease the need for outside assistance, streamline the development process, and shorten wait times for essential resources.

Typical Self-Service Elements and Their Advantages

Self-service platforms often come with a number of features that improve and expedite development processes. The following lists several popular self-service choices along with the advantages they offer to both businesses and developers:

Giving developers the ability to provision resources like storage, virtual machines, and containers without depending on operations or IT teams is known as "resource provisioning." By cutting down on wait periods, developers are able to begin working on their projects right away.

Environment Configuration and Management: Enabling developers to set up their own testing and development environments to as closely resemble production as feasible. This guarantees uniformity and reduces "environment drift," which occurs when environmental variations result in unforeseen problems.

The provision of self-service access to code repositories, version control systems, and branch management facilitates independent code management and collaboration among developers. Better teamwork and quicker iteration cycles are made possible by this.

With the help of automated build and deployment tools, developers may start builds and deploy without requiring operational support. By streamlining the continuous integration and deployment process, these automated systems guarantee quicker and more dependable releases.

Dashboards for monitoring and observability: Giving

developers access to real-time monitoring and observability tools enables them to recognize, debug, and fix problems on their own. These dashboards offer insightful information on resource consumption, system performance, and possible bottlenecks.

Self-Service Platforms' Advantages for Developers

By decreasing reliance on other teams, speeding up setup times, and doing away with several manual procedures, self-service platforms increase developer productivity. Additional advantages consist of:

The ability of developers to swiftly modify environments or resources to meet evolving project requirements results in **increased agility,** which speeds up problem-solving and iteration.

Enhanced Developer Satisfaction: A more positive, satisfying work environment is produced when developers are given autonomy and workflow friction is decreased.

Decreased Bottlenecks: Self-service platforms ease the

burden on operations and IT teams by enabling developers to handle their own resources.

5.2 Lessening Operations' Dependency on Developers

Reducing developers' reliance on operations staff is one of the main goals of self-service platforms. For tasks like resource provisioning, application deployment, and environment configuration, traditional development workflows frequently call for close collaboration with operations teams. Both developers and operations staff may become frustrated as a result of this dependence on operations, which slows down development cycles and causes bottlenecks.

Reducing Obstacles and Boosting Independence

Several crucial tactics that boost independence and productivity among development teams might help lessen the reliance of developers on operations:

Automated Infrastructure Management: Developers can spin up environments and distribute resources as needed using self-service platforms that have automated infrastructure management. Development cycles are shortened as a result of the removal of the requirement to wait for operations teams to manually provide infrastructure.

Predefined Templates and Configurations: Self-service platforms eliminate the need for developers to communicate with operations to configure environments by offering predefined templates for typical configurations and deployment setups. While enabling developers to continue without requiring a lot of setup, templates aid in standardizing procedures.

Implementing role-based access controls, or RBAC, in self-service platforms guarantees that developers have the access they need to complete their jobs without needing operations' permission for each action. This maintains security and compliance while boosting autonomy.

Self-Serve CI/CD Pipelines: Developers can automate their build and deployment processes with the help of Continuous Integration/Continuous Deployment (CI/CD) pipelines set up within self-service platforms. Developers may provide updates more frequently and react to changes faster if they take control of these pipelines themselves.

Reducing Developer Reliance on Operations Has Benefits

Reducing reliance on operations has various strategic benefits:

Quicker Time-to-Market: Self-service platforms allow developers to release updates and code modifications more rapidly, which shortens the time it takes to launch new features and improvements.

Enhanced Cooperation: Self-service features allow developers and operations to operate more autonomously, which lessens disputes over infrastructure management and resource distribution.

Operational Efficiency: Instead of responding to the same provisioning requests, operations teams may concentrate on high-value tasks like infrastructure optimization and scalability.

5.3 Harmonizing Governance and Freedom

Self-service platforms provide developers more latitude, but it's important to strike a balance between freedom and control. Operational hazards, security flaws, and inconsistencies can result from excessive autonomy without supervision. Therefore, platform engineering must guarantee that self-service platforms offer flexibility without sacrificing organizational norms, security, or compliance.

Offering Adaptability while Preserving Standards and Security

Platform engineers must put in place safeguards that provide flexibility without compromising governance in order to achieve this balance, which calls for careful design. The following are some methods to accomplish this:

Implementing Guardrails with Policy-as-Code: The

platform allows for the codification of policies that enforce operational, security, and compliance criteria. Organizations can enforce rules about resource use, access control, and environment setups by using policy-as-code technologies like Open Policy Agent (OPA). Developers are allowed to work within specified parameters that guarantee corporate compliance by incorporating these regulations into the platform.

Standardization of Key Resources and Services: Preconfigured environments, security protocols, and authorized third-party integrations are examples of standardized resources and services that self-service platforms ought to offer. While providing developers with the freedom to create within predetermined parameters, this standardization encourages uniformity.

Permissions and Role-Based Access Controls (RBAC): RBAC allows for fine-grained control over what each team or developer may view and alter. Platform engineers may guarantee that developers have the resources they require without gaining unauthorized access to sensitive systems or altering them by carefully specifying roles and permissions.

Audit Logging and Monitoring: Logging and monitoring features that trace activity within the platform should be included in self-service platforms. Platform engineering teams may maintain supervision and promptly resolve any irregularities or possible problems by keeping an eye on who has access to what resources and recording changes in real-time.

The advantages of striking a balance between governance and freedom

Productivity and security are improved when developer autonomy and control are properly balanced. This strategy helps the company in the following ways:

Enhanced Security and Compliance: Even in a self-service setting, guardrails guarantee that security procedures and compliance measures are consistently implemented.

Decreased Risk of Operational Issues: Platform

engineering lowers the possibility of mistakes and inconsistencies in production environments by upholding standards for resource utilization, configuration, and deployment procedures.

Improved Developer Productivity: By adhering to best practices and operating with more autonomy, developers can optimize workflows without sacrificing operational stability.

Scalable Management: Organizations can more readily scale self-service platforms to accommodate larger development teams without raising risks by implementing policy-based safeguards and standardizing resources.

By giving developers access to tools, lowering dependencies, and encouraging a healthy balance between autonomy and governance, platform engineering may greatly improve the developer experience through self-service platforms. In addition to streamlining processes, these platforms foster an empowering environment that boosts general productivity within the company, speeds up application delivery, and frees up developers to concentrate on innovation.

CHAPTER 6

PLATFORM ENGINEERING SECURITY AND COMPLIANCE

Platform engineering views security and compliance as essential components that support the platform's dependability, integrity, and credibility rather than as afterthoughts. Maintaining security and regulatory compliance becomes both essential and difficult as businesses use more intricate and dynamic technologies. Platform engineering can support strong defenses while streamlining compliance procedures and preserving operational agility when done with a security-first mentality. This chapter explores how platform engineering teams may create a comprehensive framework for safe, legal operations by implementing security-by-design principles, automating compliance checks, enforcing policies, and managing access through Identity and Access Management (IAM) systems.

6.1 Platform Engineering Security-by-Design

Instead of addressing security reactively, security-by-design is a proactive strategy that integrates security into each step of the platform engineering process. Platform engineering teams can stop vulnerabilities from appearing later in the deployment process by incorporating security measures from the beginning. This strategy fosters a security-conscious culture within the engineering team while lowering risk, increasing resilience, and lowering the possibility of expensive security events.

Including Security at All Platform Design Levels

A thorough security-by-design approach guarantees that security is integrated into every platform layer. To do this, follow these crucial steps:

Threat Modeling and Risk Assessment: Teams can find possible vulnerabilities and evaluate risks based on various attack vectors by conducting threat modeling sessions throughout the design process. This procedure aids in building a secure architecture from the ground up and provides guidance for implementing the proper controls.

Secure Code Practices: Common vulnerabilities like SQL injection and cross-site scripting (XSS) are lessened by implementing secure coding standards, which include input validation, error handling, and avoiding hard-coded credentials. To identify such problems early, automated scanning techniques and frequent code reviews should be used to enforce secure programming practices.

Encryption and Data Protection: Protecting sensitive data requires both in-transit and at-rest data security. Platform engineers should make sure that robust encryption protocols (like TLS and AES) are used and that encryption keys are handled safely. This complies with regulations and guards against illegal data access.

Network Segmentation and Micro-Segmentation: Network segmentation limits lateral movement in the event of a breach and reduces the scope of access by dividing a network into smaller zones. By segregating workloads within virtualized or containerized environments, micro-segmentation expands on this idea and stops attackers from freely moving throughout the system.

Automated Security Testing and Continuous Monitoring: Code is inspected for vulnerabilities before production by integrating automated security testing tools, such as static and dynamic application security testing (SAST and DAST), into the CI/CD pipeline. Detecting and reducing hazards as they appear is further aided by ongoing monitoring via real-time alerts and analytics.

The advantages of security-by-design

There are numerous important advantages to the security-by-design concept:

By proactively addressing security in the platform engineering process, vulnerabilities are decreased, sensitive data is protected, and the likelihood of breaches is decreased.

Lower Costs: It is significantly less expensive to address security flaws during the design stage than it is to do so after deployment.

Enhanced Compliance: Organizations can more readily comply with regulatory requirements when security controls are integrated, which lessens the workload associated with audits and compliance inspections.

6.2 Automation of Compliance and Enforcement of Policies

For platforms to satisfy corporate rules and regulatory standards without putting a strain on development and operations teams, compliance automation and policy enforcement are essential. Platform developers may streamline auditing, preserve uniform governance, and lower human error by automating compliance checks and incorporating policy-as-code.

Streamlining Auditing and Compliance Checks

Particularly in settings where software release cycles are quick, compliance requirements can be intricate and difficult to monitor. Tools and procedures for ongoing system monitoring and validation against regulatory standards are introduced by compliance automation.

The use of policy-as-code enables the programmatic definition, enforcement, and monitoring of compliance policies. Organizations can ensure compliance with regulatory standards without manual oversight by codifying rules that automatically apply to settings, deployments, and infrastructure using tools like Open Policy Agent (OPA) or HashiCorp Sentinel.

Automated Compliance Checks: To make sure that resources, configurations, and code comply with legal standards (such as GDPR and HIPAA), compliance automation systems regularly scan them. Real-time automated checks find non-compliant parts, warning teams of problems before they affect production.

The integration of continuous auditing into platform operations results in real-time compliance reports, which assist teams in maintaining an accurate compliance record. Because the necessary documents and paperwork are created and saved automatically, this streamlines the audit process.

Immutable Infrastructure: This type of infrastructure creates a consistent environment that facilitates compliance by replacing components instead of altering them. Immutable deployments guarantee that every deployment stays in its conforming condition by minimizing configuration drift.

The advantages of automation for compliance

Significant operational benefits are offered by automated policy enforcement and compliance checks:

Efficiency: Teams can concentrate on other objectives since automated compliance eliminates the requirement for manual verification.

Accuracy and Consistency: By reducing the possibility of human error, automated systems uphold a uniform compliance level throughout the platform.

Scalability: Compliance automation grows with businesses, guaranteeing that new systems and resources automatically conform to rules and regulations.

6.3 Management of Identity and Access (IAM)

Any security and compliance framework must include Identity and Access Management (IAM), which establishes and regulates who has access to what platform resources. Good IAM procedures are necessary to lower the risk of unwanted access, improve overall security, and guarantee that only authorized individuals can interact with sensitive data and vital systems.

Maintaining Appropriate User Authorization and Authentication

IAM includes a number of essential procedures and resources for controlling user identities, enforcing access restrictions, and keeping an eye on user behavior. Here are some essential IAM tactics:

Role-Based Access Control (RBAC): RBAC gives users authorization according to their position in the company. By using this method, administrators can limit access to resources based on job duties, hence reducing exposure to sensitive information and features.

Requiring multi-factor authentication (MFA) gives an extra layer of security, especially when it comes to accessing high-risk parts of the platform. By using a second authentication factor, like a one-time code or biometric verification, MFA makes sure that even if an attacker manages to get their hands on a password, they will be unable to access the system.

By enabling users to authenticate only once and access numerous apps or systems, Single Sign-On (SSO) centralized access management. SSO lowers the possibility of weak or reused passwords, streamlines the user experience, and lessens password fatigue.

Least Privilege Access: By putting the least privilege principle into practice, users are given the bare minimum of access required to do their tasks. By restricting the extent of access to sensitive resources, this strategy lowers the attack surface.

The ability to authenticate users across numerous, reliable external domains is made possible by identity federation. Because it allows for secure access while upholding stringent identification restrictions, this procedure is crucial for businesses collaborating with partners or outside providers.

IAM Technologies and Tools

In platform engineering contexts, a number of IAM tools and technologies support the enforcement of identity and access controls:

The management of permissions, roles, and access policies in a cloud environment is made simpler by native IAM solutions that interact with platform services, which are provided by cloud providers such as AWS, Azure, and Google Cloud.

Directory Services: Platform teams can simplify user and role management across systems by utilizing directory services like Microsoft Active Directory or LDAP, which offer centralized user management and authentication capabilities.

Access Management for APIs: API gateways can add an extra degree of security by enforcing access controls for users and apps interacting with APIs. This prevents unauthorized access to platform resources.

The advantages of having a strong IAM strategy

Several important advantages come from integrating a thorough IAM strategy into platform engineering:

Enhanced Security: By restricting access to important resources, IAM lowers the possibility of breaches and illegal data access.

Streamlined Compliance: By implementing access controls and offering audit trails that monitor user behavior, IAM systems assist businesses in adhering to legal obligations.

Enhanced Operational Efficiency: IAM makes access management easier, enabling administrators to effortlessly handle roles and permissions when teams and platforms change.

Platform engineering teams can build environments that are safe, compliant, and resilient by automating compliance checks, integrating security at every level, and putting in place a robust IAM framework. In addition to safeguarding company assets, this proactive strategy builds stakeholder and customer trust, which eventually creates a stable, safe basis for expansion.

CHAPTER 7

EXPANDING TEAMS: SCALING AND IMPROVING PLATFORMS

Platform engineering must change as teams grow in size and project complexity to satisfy these new requirements. In addition to scaling to handle increasing user and project counts, a well-designed platform guarantees peak performance, economical resource consumption, and robust governance. This chapter examines the ideas and methods necessary to develop a high-performing, scalable platform for varied and expanding teams. We look at methods for modifying platforms to accommodate a range of project sizes, maximizing resource use for cost and performance effectiveness, and putting governance principles into place to preserve operational consistency and compliance.

7.1 Scalability of the Platform for Diverse Teams

Platforms must scale to meet a range of project sizes,

complexities, and technical needs in order to serve diverse and growing teams. The ability of a platform to increase in capability and capacity in response to increasing team demands and user demand is known as platform scalability. This flexibility guarantees that resources are available when projects call for them, minimizing bottlenecks and allowing teams to continue producing at any size.

Platforms can be modified to accommodate a range of project sizes and complexity.

In platform engineering, scalability refers to structural modifications that enable systems to increase in both performance and capacity. In order to achieve scalability, a platform must be able to accommodate increases in load, complexity, and user diversity without experiencing a drop in user experience or performance.

Horizontal and Vertical Scaling: Two essential methods for boosting capacity are horizontal scaling, which involves adding more instances of resources, and vertical scaling, which involves giving current resources more power. Containerized environments, for example, may swiftly launch additional instances to handle demand spikes, which is especially helpful for a variety of project requirements.

Microservices Architecture: Teams can grow individual components independently when designing platforms with a microservices architecture. This makes it perfect for teams working on several projects with different needs because it allows some services to be grown as a project expands without impacting the system as a whole.

Dynamic Load Balancing: Dynamic load balancers make sure that resources are distributed effectively throughout the platform as user demand varies. This keeps any one server or element from becoming overloaded, which is especially crucial for bigger teams with plenty of activity.

A single platform may support numerous teams or projects while preserving data separation thanks to multi-tenancy support. Multi-tenancy lowers expenses while preserving scalability for businesses with various teams by enabling each team to have its own environment on a shared platform.

A Scalable Platform's Advantages

A scalable platform offers a number of important benefits:

Enhanced Team Productivity: Teams can concentrate on their primary responsibilities by utilizing a high-performance, responsive platform that adjusts to their evolving requirements.

Decreased Operational Costs: As the platform expands, operational costs are kept to a minimum because effective scalability frequently translates into efficient resource usage.

Scalable platforms facilitate quick iterations, testing, and deployment, allowing teams to experiment and innovate without being limited by platform constraints. This results in **Enhanced Flexibility and Innovation.**

7.2 Enhancing Efficiency and Utilizing Resources

Maintaining platform efficiency and controlling expenses

require optimizing performance and resource utilization, particularly in cloud systems where resources are invoiced on usage. A key component of platform engineering for expanding teams, efficient resource management optimizes platform responsiveness, improves user experience, and balances costs with real resource demands.

Effective Cloud Resource Utilization and Cost Control

Resource optimization is the smart use of network, storage, and computer resources to provide teams the performance they require without going over budget. The following are fundamental procedures for platform resource optimization:

Instances of Autoscaling and Right-Sizing: While right-sizing guarantees that instances are appropriately sized for their task, autoscaling automatically modifies resources in response to demand. Platforms can cut down on wasteful resource usage and limit expenses by scaling resources up or down as necessary.

Cost-Effective Storage Solutions: Choosing the right

storage tiers according to data access patterns is part of storage optimization. High-performance disks can be utilized to store frequently accessed data, while more affordable, long-term storage options can be used to store archive or infrequently used data, greatly lowering storage costs.

Effective cost allocation and usage tracking are made possible by assigning project-specific identities to resources. Cost allocation reports encourage accountability and cost transparency by assisting teams in identifying projects that require a lot of resources and modifying their use accordingly.

With serverless architecture, developers may run code without having to provision or manage servers. This makes it possible to use serverless computing for variable loads. Because resources are only used when code is executed, it's especially advantageous for workloads with fluctuating demand and can result in significant cost reductions.

Monitoring and Performance Tuning: Monitoring tools offer up-to-date information on application performance, resource consumption, and any bottlenecks. Platform engineers can proactively modify configurations, optimize code, and guarantee seamless operation by establishing alarms and examining performance data.

Advantages of Optimal Resource Utilization

Resource optimization is necessary to build a high-performance, reasonably priced platform:

Lower Cloud Expenses: By adjusting resources to match real demand, overspending may be avoided and ROI can be increased.

Enhanced Application Performance: By lowering latency and speeding up reaction times, performance optimization makes the user experience more seamless.

Effective resource management facilitates platform expansion, enabling teams to grow without incurring rapidly rising expenses.

7.3 Policy Management and Platform Governance

Implementing governance controls that guarantee responsible platform usage, adherence to industry norms, and alignment with corporate standards becomes crucial as platforms and teams develop. Platform governance creates the rules and regulations required to regulate platform use, enforce adherence, and preserve a high level of operational uniformity.

Creating Explicit Guidelines for Platform Usage and Adherence

Developing and implementing policies for compliance, resource utilization, data processing, and access are all part of effective platform governance. In addition to lowering the possibility of security issues, clear regulations simplify platform operations and provide teams the confidence to operate within predetermined parameters.

Policies for Access Control: Role-based access control (RBAC) ensures that users can only access the resources they require. Establishing roles and permissions promotes adherence to data security laws and helps stop unwanted access.

The implementation of resource quotas and limits lowers the risk of service deterioration and unforeseen expenses by preventing teams from using excessive amounts of resources. Quotas promote equitable use among teams and ethical resource consumption.

Auditing and Compliance: Adhering to industry rules like HIPAA and GDPR requires compliance policies. Automated auditing to monitor data handling, user access, and resource utilization should be part of platform governance. This reduces the possibility of regulatory infractions while also making compliance reporting easier.

Environmental Standardization: Maintaining standard settings for environments encourages uniformity and lowers variability, which might result in mistakes or security flaws. For instance, teams can easily construct standardized, compliant environments that follow company norms by leveraging Infrastructure as Code (IaC) templates.

Policy-as-Code: Organizations can automate policy enforcement and guarantee consistent adherence to governance requirements by declaring policies as code. Real-time configuration, deployment, and resource monitoring is possible with policy-as-code solutions, which can also automatically identify and fix policy infractions.

The advantages of platform governance

A platform with good governance is safe, legal, and well-run:

The implementation of governance policies lowers the risk of expensive compliance violations by establishing controls that safeguard sensitive data and guarantee conformity to legal standards.

Operational Efficiency: Teams may concentrate on higher-value work since automated enforcement and clear policies minimize the manual labor needed to maintain compliance and control.

Trust and Reliability: Governance increases platform trust since teams are aware that they are operating in a safe and regulated setting, which promotes an accountable and effective work culture.

Platform engineering can provide expanding teams with the resources and flexibility they require while preserving cost-effectiveness, performance, and compliance by concentrating on scalability, optimization, and governance. A platform that has been properly optimized and managed encourages a culture of accountability and creativity, enabling teams to produce superior solutions that propel organizational expansion.

CHAPTER 8

ASSESSING PLATFORM ENGINEERING INITIATIVES' PERFORMANCE

Clear and measurable metrics are necessary for platform engineering to prove its worth. In addition to increasing team productivity and assisting teams in making data-driven decisions for ongoing improvement, effective measurement shows how effectively platform engineering projects match business objectives. This chapter explores how to demonstrate the return on investment (ROI) that platform engineering activities provide to a business, the significance of feedback loops, and the key metrics used to assess platform engineering performance. Every part offers guidance on how to create a strong measurement framework that will promote platform engineering initiatives' accountability, improvement, and expansion.

8.1 Crucial Indicators for Platform Engineering Achievement

Identifying and monitoring important metrics is essential to evaluating the results of platform engineering projects. These indicators offer insight into platform dependability, development pace, and operational efficiency. Platform developers and other stakeholders can better understand what is effective and where changes are required by measuring these aspects.

Key Performance Indicators

Organizations usually concentrate on a number of key performance indicators (KPIs) in order to measure platform engineering progress in a comprehensive manner. Every metric offers a different viewpoint on the efficacy of the platform:

The time it takes for code changes to go from development to production is measured by the **Time-to-Deploy (TTD)** metric. An effective, well-optimized pipeline that enables teams to swiftly roll out updates, fixes, and new features is indicated by a quicker time-to-deploy. Reducing TTD improves responsiveness to market demands by increasing agility and minimizing the time lag between code production and user delivery.

Mean-Time-to-Repair (MTTR): MTTR calculates the typical amount of time needed to fix system or platform problems. A lower MTTR indicates a comprehensive monitoring system and an efficient incident response mechanism, which facilitates prompt issue detection and resolution. In platform engineering, MTTR minimization is essential for preserving platform dependability and lessening the effect of outages on user productivity and development.

Feedback Loop Duration: This measure measures the interval between user input and platform modifications that can be implemented. Feedback loops guarantee that platform enhancements meet user requirements. Platform engineers can swiftly resolve issues, streamline processes, and maintain platform alignment with changing needs by cutting down on this time.

Deployment Frequency: One of the most important indicators of agility is how quickly teams release updates or new code to production. Rapid innovation is made possible by streamlined procedures and reduced friction in the development pipeline, which are indicated by higher deployment frequencies. This measure is especially helpful for evaluating how well the platform can accommodate rapid development cycles.

Platform Reliability and Uptime: In platform engineering, reliability is crucial since downtime can cause delays in important releases and impede developer productivity. Monitoring uptime, issue frequency, and incident severity offers valuable information about the platform's stability and the success of reliability-focused programs.

Extending Measures Outside of Operations

Platform engineering success might not be adequately captured by operational measures alone. A more comprehensive view is provided by complementary business-oriented metrics:

Developer Productivity and Satisfaction: Regular developer surveys can yield qualitative information on the effectiveness and usability of platforms. Feedback on pain locations can direct future changes, and high satisfaction levels are frequently associated with high productivity.

Teams can determine which tools and workflows are most useful by tracking the adoption rate of particular platform features. Prioritizing more development in areas that provide the greatest value to users can be aided by this data.

8.2 Continuous Improvement and Feedback Loops

For any platform engineering strategy to be successful, feedback loops are essential. By guaranteeing that user input both explicit (such as comments and surveys) and implicit (such as usage data and behavioral patterns) is regularly integrated into platform upgrades, a feedback loop promotes ongoing improvement. In addition to maintaining the platform's relevance to changing needs, this iterative approach promotes an agile and transparent culture.

Continuous Feedback Is Essential for Platform Improvement

Platform engineers run the danger of developing products that fall short of user requirements and usability standards in the absence of continuous input. Constant feedback systems guarantee that the platform stays responsive and focused on the user:

Gathering Explicit Feedback: Surveys, user interviews, and regularly planned feedback sessions can yield useful information on workflow issues and developer satisfaction. To get a comprehensive picture of platform performance, input should be obtained from a wide spectrum of users, including developers, operations teams, and even non-technical stakeholders.

Tracking Implicit Feedback: In addition to direct feedback, users' interactions with the platform might provide insightful information. Metrics that show where users are inefficient include feature adoption rates, time spent on particular tasks, and workflow friction spots. Platform engineers can prioritize usability and complexity-reducing modifications by examining implicit input.

Including Feedback in the Development Cycle: The platform's development lifecycle should include feedback as a fundamental component. Platform engineers can iteratively address changing needs and preferences by incorporating feedback sessions throughout every sprint or release.

The advantages of adopting a continuous improvement approach

Organizations can create a responsive, user-centered platform by routinely gathering and reacting to feedback:

Increased User Satisfaction: A platform that adapts to user feedback is more likely to satisfy developer requirements, which raises user satisfaction and boosts productivity.

Decreased Development Waste: Teams may concentrate on projects that have a direct impact on user experience since engineers are prevented from investing in features or workflows that don't add value by constant feedback.

Enhanced Flexibility and Agility: It is simpler to adjust to changes, whether they originate from internal changes in corporate strategy or external market needs, when regular feedback loops and iterative improvements are implemented.

8.3 Showing Platform Engineering's Return on Investment

Organizations must quantify and convey the return on investment (ROI) of platform engineering efforts in order to support them. ROI demonstrations assist stakeholders in comprehending the observable advantages that platform engineering offers the company, such as increased agility, lower expenses, and productivity increases.

Exhibiting Increases in Productivity and Efficiency

Platform engineering ROI measurement necessitates a combination of quantitative and qualitative evaluations that connect platform enhancements to organizational results:

Determining Productivity Increases: Developer productivity is directly impacted by metrics such as shorter time-to-deploy, more frequent deployments, and quicker incident response. Platform enhancements that lower TTD by 30%, for example, enable developers to deliver features more quickly, resulting in quantifiable time savings that provide value.

Cost Savings by Resource Optimization: Especially in cloud contexts, platform engineering frequently entails resource optimization. Organizations can measure cost savings and show effective spending by comparing resource use before and after platform optimizations. Improved load balancing, better infrastructure use, or less reliance on pricey third-party technologies could all contribute to these savings.

Improved Agility and Innovation Speed: New features and products reach the market more quickly thanks to quicker deployment and shorter feedback loops. Stakeholders can better understand how platform engineering increases organizational agility and meets competitive expectations by seeing that it supports a high deployment frequency.

Developing a Platform Engineering Business Case

The impact of platform engineering investment must be framed in terms of business value in order to make a strong argument for it. When stakeholders see how platform engineering advances strategic objectives, they are more inclined to support projects.

Connect platform engineering measurements to more general business KPIs in order to link platform engineering to business outcomes. For instance, demonstrating how a shorter time-to-deploy allows for faster product releases emphasizes the influence of platform engineering on activities that generate money.

Using Case Studies and Success Stories: You can make a compelling argument by providing actual instances of how platform engineering resolved particular problems or increased productivity. The platform's worth is demonstrated by case studies that show measurable increases in productivity, cost savings, or user satisfaction.

Continuous Platform Performance Reporting: A regular reporting schedule on important indicators and accomplishments promotes openness and demonstrates steady advancement. A real-time overview of platform performance is provided by dashboards that measure parameters like MTTR, TTD, and feedback loop duration. This makes it simple to keep an eye on and share continuous success.

The Advantages of ROI Demonstration

The company gains by tracking and sharing platform engineering's return on investment in a number of ways.

Secures Stakeholder Buy-In: Leadership support is fostered by clearly demonstrating ROI, which raises the possibility of sustained investment and resources for platform activities.

Strategic planning is guided by ROI criteria, which assist teams in concentrating on high-impact projects and guarantee that platform engineering resources are directed toward the most valuable endeavors.

Promotes Accountability and Transparency: By concentrating on ROI, teams are held responsible for producing quantifiable outcomes, fostering trust within the company and highlighting the significance of platform engineering.

All things considered, evaluating the effectiveness of platform engineering projects using pertinent metrics, ongoing feedback loops, and ROI analysis offers a clear picture of how the platform affects cost savings, productivity, and efficiency. Platform engineering may provide long-term value that complements corporate goals and user needs by keeping a laser-like focus on data-driven enhancements.

CHAPTER 9

OVERCOMING PLATFORM ENGINEERING DIFFICULTIES

Platform engineering has the potential to revolutionize software development processes by increasing scalability, dependability, and efficiency. Adopting platform engineering is not without its difficulties, though, just like any other innovation. Organizations face a variety of challenges that can prevent successful adoption, ranging from financial constraints to technological difficulties and cultural resistance. This chapter examines typical issues encountered when adopting platform engineering, offers advice on how to fix technical problems, and presents case studies of effective implementations to show how actual businesses have dealt with these issues. Businesses can optimize their platform engineering endeavors by comprehending and resolving these issues.

9.1 Typical Barriers to Adoption of Platform Engineering

Platform engineering necessitates changes in procedures, equipment, and frequent attitude. Transitional challenges are common, particularly when procedures and existing teams need to adjust to new methods.

Opposition to Change

One of the biggest obstacles to implementing platform engineering is resistance to change. Adopting a centralized platform strategy may be difficult for team members used to traditional development procedures. Among the causes of resistance are:

Anxiety about Job Redundancy: Operations staff and engineers may be concerned that automation and self-service platforms would render their positions obsolete. This anxiety can be lessened with openness and instruction on how platform engineering frees up teams to concentrate on higher-value work.

It's possible that certain team members are not aware of platform engineering concepts like infrastructure-as-code (IaC), automated CI/CD pipelines, and internal development platforms (IDPs). Enhancing buy-in can be achieved by providing thorough training and emphasizing the advantages of efficient processes.

Comfort with Existing Processes: Teams may become comfortable with long-standing procedures. They may see the benefits of change by seeing how platform engineering addresses typical issues like cross-team dependencies or deployment delays.

Restrictions on the Budget

Adoption of platform engineering may be impacted by financial constraints, especially if the project calls for expenditures on new equipment, infrastructure, or skilled workers:

Expense of New Tools and Infrastructure: For automation, monitoring, and deployment, platform engineering frequently calls for specialized tools.

Businesses may encounter early financial obstacles, but presenting these costs as investments with possible returns on investment in terms of cost savings and productivity can support the development of a business case.

Funding for Training and Skill Development: Upskilling employees is often a necessary part of adopting platform engineering. Setting aside money for mentorship and training initiatives can ease the transition and lessen conflict brought on by skill disparities.

Limited Resources for Pilot Programs: Platform engineering can be shown to be beneficial through small-scale pilot programs that don't require a large upfront expenditure. By demonstrating success in a small area, organizations can support additional financing.

Knowledge Limitations and Skill Gaps

One potential obstacle is the specific knowledge needed for platform engineering:

Lack of Platform Engineering experience: Since

platform engineering integrates knowledge from operations, development, and architecture, it might be difficult to locate staff with this hybrid experience. First skill shortages can be filled by upskilling through training and using seasoned advisors.

Unfamiliarity with Emerging Tools and Practices: Teams may feel overburdened by the quick changes in best practices and tools. Establishing a culture of lifelong learning and scheduling time to experiment with new tools guarantees that teams stay current and flexible.

Organizations should take proactive measures to foster a platform engineering adoption environment and establish the foundation for more seamless integration and long-term success by recognizing and resolving these typical roadblocks.

9.2 Technical Issues and Their Fixes

Platform engineering has many technical difficulties in addition to organizational ones. These challenges are frequently brought on by the difficulties of integrating several systems, preserving low latency, and guaranteeing cross-platform compatibility. Resolving these issues is essential to providing a dependable, stable platform that satisfies user requirements.

Difficulties with Integration

Effective platform engineering is based on the smooth integration of different tools and systems. But difficulties can occur, particularly in settings with a variety of legacy systems and cloud-based apps:

Inconsistent APIs: Integration may be hampered by differences in API documentation and design. Organizations can address this by standardizing API designs and managing and streamlining communications across services with the use of solutions like API gateways.

Legacy Systems and new technologies: It's possible that legacy systems aren't compatible enough to work with cloud-native architectures and new technologies. Without a complete redesign, legacy systems can interface with modern infrastructure by using middleware solutions or custom adapters.

Data Silos: Information transfer between systems may be hampered by disconnected data silos. Centralizing access to vital information through the use of shared data lakes or data integration layers helps promote more seamless platform interoperability.

Optimization of Latency and Performance

Effective, real-time operations must be supported by platform engineering without causing performance snags. Reduced productivity, a bad developer experience, and slower deployment times can all result from high latency:

Platform workflows may be slowed down by high network latency, particularly in distributed systems. Latency can be reduced by employing strategies including caching frequently accessed data, streamlining network routing, and utilizing content delivery networks (CDNs) for worldwide access.

Database Optimization: A major cause of slowness is

frequent databases. Data-intensive applications can have faster response times by optimizing database queries, indexing frequently requested data, and putting caching technologies in place.

Load Balancing and Autoscaling: Applying load balancers and autoscaling to applications with varying demand guarantees that resources adapt to workload variations in real time, preventing performance problems during periods of high usage.

Compatibility Problems

Another technical problem in platform engineering is ensuring compatibility across various platforms, environments, and devices:

Cross-Platform Compatibility: Extensive testing and frequently unique solutions are needed to ensure that tools and services function across many operating systems and environments. Through the creation of uniform environments across deployments, containerization with tools like Docker helps simplify cross-platform compatibility.

Version Control and Dependency Management: Compatibility problems may arise from dependencies between various tool and library versions. Reducing conflicts and offering centralized control over program versions are two benefits of using dependency managers and container registries.

Device and Browser Compatibility: Cross-platform and cross-browser compatibility is crucial for user-facing interfaces. Testing for browser compatibility and using responsive design concepts can help guarantee a seamless cross-platform user experience.

9.3 Successful Platform Engineering Case Studies

Case studies from the real world offer insightful insights into how businesses successfully navigate platform engineering obstacles. By looking at how these businesses overcame challenges, we can learn useful tactics for putting platform engineering into practice.

Case Study 1: Overcoming Financial Institution Legacy System Challenges

Integrating historical systems using a contemporary platform engineering approach presented difficulties for a significant financial institution. Their outdated infrastructure was incompatible with containerization and contemporary CI/CD tools. To deal with this:

The organization implemented a hybrid architecture that bridges older systems with more recent microservices through the use of middleware. They minimized disruptions to current workflows while enabling consistent integration through the use of API gateways and the gradual containerization of legacy apps.

As a result, they were able to gradually update their infrastructure, enhancing system interoperability and facilitating the implementation of automated deployment procedures without requiring a complete redesign.

Case Study No. 2: Enhancing Developer Autonomy in a Technology Startup

A digital startup realized that deployment and innovation were being slowed down by developers' reliance on operations teams. To lessen bottlenecks and boost agility:

Solution: They gave developers more control over their development environment by implementing a self-service internal developer platform (IDP) that automated CI/CD pipelines and infrastructure provisioning. They ensured compliance while reducing errors by offering templates and predefined configurations.

Result: The self-service platform shortened deployment times, empowered developers to work independently, and cut down on reliance on operations by 60%. This allowed for quicker feature delivery and increased overall productivity.

Case Study 3: Cutting Cloud Expenses in an Online Store

An online retailer aimed to lower cloud costs while improving the scalability and performance of its platform. Due to improper resource allocation, the platform was suffering from rising expenses and increased delay.

Solution: The technical team improved database queries, added caching to speed up response times, and put in place an autoscaling policy that dynamically modified resources based on demand. Additionally, they implemented a cost-monitoring program that detected unused resources and tracked cloud consumption.

A better customer experience was achieved as a result of these initiatives, which reduced cloud spending by 30%, improved response times by 20%, and increased platform resilience during periods of high shopping demand.

Important Lessons Learned from Case Studies

These case studies demonstrate a number of crucial approaches to resolving platform engineering issues:

Gradual Modernization: By using a hybrid strategy, businesses can update legacy systems without causing significant disruptions or large upfront expenditures.

Self-service solutions that decrease reliance on operations boost developer autonomy and expedite deployment schedules, hence empowering developers.

Cost Optimization: Autoscaling and cloud resource monitoring cut down on wasteful spending, improving performance and budget allocation.

Organizations may successfully manage the difficulties of platform engineering adoption by comprehending typical roadblocks, resolving technical issues, and taking inspiration from successful case studies. These insights enable teams to create robust, scalable, and effective platforms that benefit developers and advance overarching company goals.

CHAPTER 10

PLATFORM ENGINEERING'S FUTURE TRENDS

Platform engineering is becoming a crucial area as the technology environment changes due to the quick development of artificial intelligence (AI), the adaptability of cloud computing, and the changing responsibilities of platform engineers. With an emphasis on AI integration, the move to hybrid and multi-cloud settings, and the growing roles and skill sets needed by platform engineers, we examine the major themes that will shape the field's future in this concluding chapter. By being aware of these patterns, engineers and organizations can better prepare for a changing future and make sure that their platforms continue to be robust, effective, and flexible.

10.1 AI and Machine Learning's Ascent on Platforms

Platform engineering is fast changing as a result of artificial intelligence (AI) and machine learning (ML), which open up new opportunities for automation, predictive analytics, and adaptive systems. These technologies can facilitate more intelligent decision-making, optimize operations, and increase platform efficiency.

Automation Driven by AI

Automation is among the most potent uses of AI in platform engineering. AI can assist engineers in concentrating on higher-value jobs that call for human ingenuity and critical thinking by automating repetitive operations. The following are important areas where AI-driven automation is having an effect:

The provisioning, monitoring, and scaling of infrastructure can be automated via AI-based solutions. This optimizes resource allocation and lowers operating costs by enabling platforms to react independently to shifting workloads.

The ability of machine learning models trained on historical data to anticipate and identify events before they happen is known as **Incident Detection and Resolution**.

These models assist in decreasing downtime and facilitating quicker reaction times when problems do occur by spotting patterns and abnormalities.

Continuous Deployment: AI-enhanced automated CI/CD pipelines can improve the resilience and efficiency of deployment procedures. Release cycles can be streamlined by using AI models to predict the effects of changes, identify possible code problems, and optimize deployment timelines.

Predictive Analytics

AI-powered predictive analytics offers priceless insights into possible problems, resource utilization, and platform performance. Predictive analytics, which uses machine learning algorithms to examine both historical and current data, can:

Forecast Demand: By using previous trends to predict demand spikes, predictive models enable platforms to plan ahead and prevent performance snags at peak periods.

Optimize Resource Allocation: AI-driven predictive analytics can help direct resource allocation decisions by forecasting future workload demands. This helps to ensure that capacity matches expected needs and prevents over-provisioning.

Identify Security Risks: Artificial intelligence systems are able to examine patterns of behavior and identify deviations that could indicate security risks. These models improve their ability to spot possible weaknesses by continuously learning from data, which raises the platform's overall security.

Organizations can attain previously unheard-of levels of automation and insight as AI and ML become more thoroughly integrated into platform engineering, resulting in systems that are more proactive, resilient, and efficient.

10.2 Multi-Cloud and Hybrid Platforms

Organizations are adopting hybrid and multi-cloud architectures at an increasing rate due to the broad use of cloud technology. With increased flexibility, redundancy, and cross-cloud compatibility, this strategy helps businesses take use of the advantages of both on-premises and cloud solutions.

Cluster Flexibility Trends

Businesses no longer depend exclusively on one cloud provider. In order to accommodate a variety of business requirements, they are instead choosing hybrid and multi-cloud platforms. Among the main causes of this tendency are:

To prevent vendor lock-in: Dependency and a lack of flexibility might result from using just one cloud service. Organizations can become more independent and change resources according to cost, performance, or regulatory requirements by dividing workloads among several clouds.

Optimizing Workloads for Cost and Performance: Various cloud providers have distinct strengths, ranging from computing and storage capacities to particular AI or ML services. Businesses can choose the most affordable or high-performing services from each provider by using a multi-cloud approach.

Ensuring Business Continuity and Redundancy: In the event of an outage, workloads can be moved between providers, making a hybrid or multi-cloud solution more resilient. The likelihood of downtime is reduced by this redundancy, which is particularly important for business continuity.

Compatibility Across Clouds

Optimizing the value of hybrid and multi-cloud platforms requires cross-cloud compatibility. Platform engineers must make sure that data and apps are accessible across various cloud environments as more businesses use this strategy. The following are some cross-cloud compatibility issues and solutions:

Standardized APIs and Interoperability: Applications can run in a variety of contexts without requiring changes thanks to standardized APIs and containerization technologies like Docker and Kubernetes. Smooth cross-cloud interactions are made possible by this standardization.

Data Compliance and Portability: It can be difficult to ensure portability and compliance when data is spread across various cloud environments. To securely and effectively manage data across clouds, platform engineers should put strong data governance and regulatory compliance frameworks in place.

Combined Monitoring and Administration: A uniform monitoring system is necessary for a multi-cloud approach in order to track expenses, security, and performance across cloud providers. Engineers can identify and fix problems more quickly thanks to centralized dashboards and monitoring systems that offer real-time visibility into the entire cloud infrastructure.

Adopting hybrid and multi-cloud platforms is a crucial trend for platform engineering in the future since it gives businesses the freedom to maximize resources, improve security, and increase scalability.

10.3 Platform Engineers' Changing Role

The function of the platform engineer changes along with platform engineering. Platform engineers must learn new skills and adjust to a shifting environment that prioritizes a balance of technical expertise, strategic thinking, and cross-functional cooperation in order to stay up with technological improvements.

The Skills of the Future for Platform Engineers

Future platform engineers will need a broad range of abilities that extend beyond conventional infrastructure management. The following core competencies are becoming more and more crucial:

Knowledge of AI and Machine Learning: Understanding AI and ML principles will be crucial as platform engineering increasingly relies on AI-driven automation and predictive analytics. The deployment, management, and optimization of AI models within the platform architecture are critical skills for platform engineers to possess.

Proficiency in cloud-native development, encompassing serverless architectures, microservices, and containerization, will be essential. These technologies serve as the cornerstone of robust, scalable platforms that can accommodate multi-cloud and hybrid settings.

Expertise in Security and Compliance: It will get harder to maintain security and compliance in a variety of settings as platforms get more complicated. To properly handle these issues, platform developers need to hone their abilities in identity management, data governance, and regulatory compliance.

Duties in a Changing Technology Environment

As platform engineers take on a more strategic role in determining platform capabilities and increasing developer efficiency, their duties are also growing. Important duties will probably consist of:

Developer Enablement: Platform engineers will put more

of an emphasis on empowering developers by creating self-service tools, streamlining processes, and offering standardized resources that enable autonomous development teams.

In order to match platform capabilities with more general company objectives, platform engineers will engage in strategic planning in addition to operational duties. This could entail looking at market trends, evaluating the scalability of the platform, and seeing areas that could want improvement.

Cross-Functional Collaboration: The development, operations, security, and compliance teams will need to work closely with platform engineers. This cross-functional strategy improves departmental platform integration and helps match platform initiatives with corporate goals.

Capacity to Adjust to New Technologies

Adaptability is becoming a key attribute of successful platform engineers due to the rapid evolution of technology. Platform engineers may promote innovation in their companies and create platforms that are not just effective but also prepared for the future by keeping abreast of developing technology.

Platform engineering will emerge as a key component of contemporary IT infrastructure due to developments in AI, cloud scalability, and a growing range of duties. Platform engineers and organizations may create robust, adaptable platforms that satisfy the demands of the modern, complex digital world and foresee those of the future by comprehending and embracing these developments.

ABOUT THE AUTHOR

 Author and thought leader in the IT field Taylor Royce is well known. He has a two-decade career and is an expert at tech trend analysis and forecasting, which enables a wide audience to understand complicated concepts.

Royce's considerable involvement in the IT industry stemmed from his passion with technology, which he developed during his computer science studies. He has extensive knowledge of the industry because of his experience in both software development and strategic consulting.

Known for his research and lucidity, he has written multiple best-selling books and contributed to esteemed tech periodicals. Translations of Royce's books throughout the world demonstrate his impact.

Royce is a well-known authority on emerging technologies and their effects on society, frequently requested as a speaker at international conferences and as a guest on tech podcasts. He promotes the development of ethical technology, emphasizing problems like data privacy and the digital divide.

In addition, with a focus on sustainable industry growth, Royce mentors upcoming tech experts and supports IT education projects. Taylor Royce is well known for his ability to combine analytical thinking with technical know-how. He sees a time when technology will ethically benefit humanity.